A Day with Animal Doctors

by Leonie Bennett

Consultant: Mitch Cronick

Credits

t=top, b=bottom, c=center, l=left, r=right, OFC=outside front cover
Corbis: 10, 11, 12–13. Superstock: 4, 5, 6, 7, 14, 15, 16, 17, 19, 20, 21.

Library of Congress Cataloging-in-Publication Data

Bennett, Leonie.
A day with animal doctors / by Leonie Bennett.
p. cm. — (I love reading)
Includes index.
ISBN 1-59716-148-9 (library binding) — ISBN 1-59716-174-8 (pbk.)
1. Veterinarians — Juvenile literature.
2. Veterinary medicine — Vocational guidance — Juvenile literature. I. Title. II. Series.

SF756.B46 2006
636.089'069 — dc22

2005030625

For more information, write to Bearport Publishing Company, Inc., 101 Fifth Avenue, Suite 6R, New York, New York 10003.
Printed in the United States of America.

1 2 3 4 5 6 7 8 9 10

The I Love Reading series was originally developed by Tick Tock Media.

CONTENTS

Animal doctors

My name's Sam.

I am an animal doctor.

I work in an animal hospital.

Julia is an animal doctor, too.

Julia and I take care of sick animals.

Animals we help

Here are some of the animals that we take care of.

Big dogs

Parrots

Guinea pigs
Small dogs
Rabbits
Cats

Tools we use

We use all of these tools in our work.

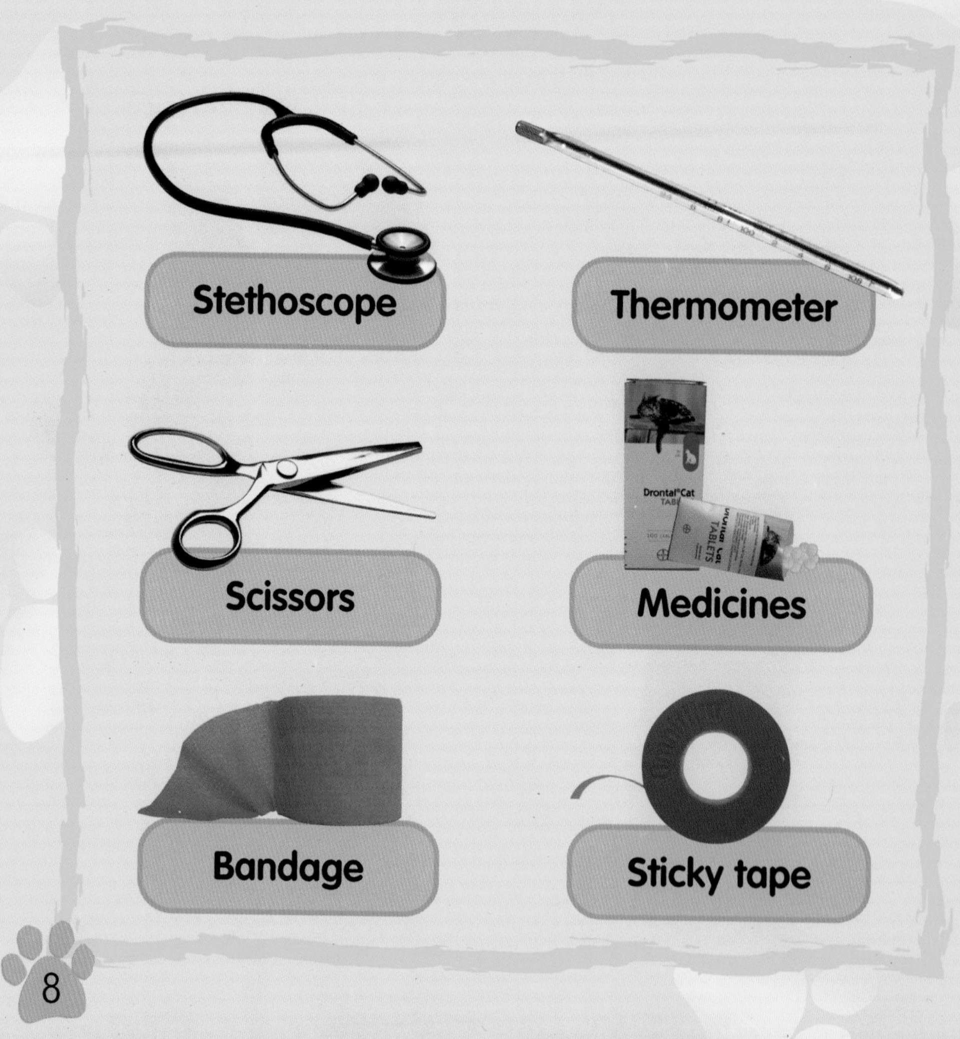

This **X ray** shows the bones in a cat's tail and legs.

We use a **syringe** to give **shots**.

Why do animals come to the animal hospital?

This dog's leg is hurt.

This rat is going to have babies.

This dog has dirty teeth.

This cat has **fleas**.

Getting shots

Many pets come to the hospital to get shots.

Shots help stop animals from getting sick.

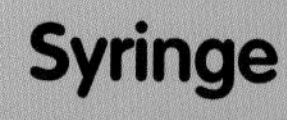

A kitten gets its first shot when it is about eight weeks old.

Alfie gets help

This dog's name is Alfie.

Alfie is not feeling well.

I feel Alfie's tummy.

I listen to his heart with a **stethoscope**.

The nurse helps.

Nurse

Stethoscope

Alfie's bad eye

I look in Alfie's ears.

I look in his eyes.

Alfie has a bad eye.

I give him a big collar.

Now Alfie can't scratch his eye.

Alfie can go home.

Good boy, Alfie!

Suzie's checkup

Suzie is an old dog.

She has come in for a checkup.

Julia uses a **thermometer** to take Suzie's temperature.

Stethoscope

Julia uses a stethoscope to listen to Suzie's heart.

Good girl, Suzie!

Julia weighs Suzie on the scale.

She looks at Suzie's teeth.

Suzie is not sick.

Good girl, Suzie!

Glossary

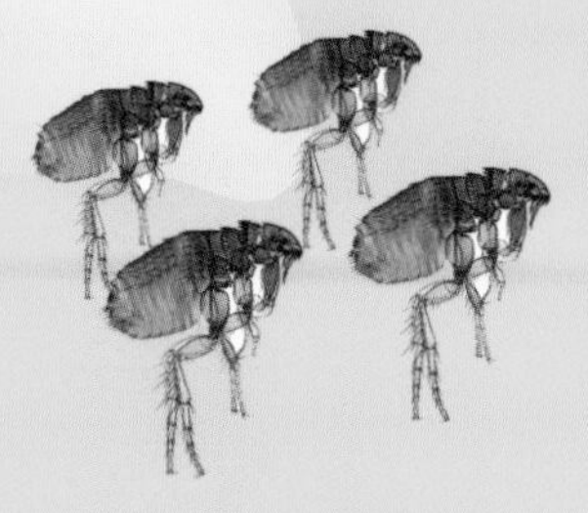

fleas (FLEEZ) small insects which live in an animal's fur

shots (SHOTS) a way of giving medicine using a needle

stethoscope (STETH-uh-*skope*) a tool used to listen to an animal's heart and lungs

syringe (suh-RINJ) a needle used to give shots

thermometer (thur-MOM-uh-tur) a tool that tells how warm or cold an animal is

X ray (EKS RAY) a special photo which shows the inside of an animal

Index

Learn More

Macken, JoAnn Early. *Veterinarian.* Stamford, CT: Weekly Reader Early Learning Library (2003).

Owen, Ann. *Caring for Your Pets: A Book About Veterinarians.* Minneapolis, MN: Picture Window Books (2003).

www.avma.org/careforanimals/default.asp

www.uga.edu/~lam/kids/day/default.html